what a mess our viscera makes

Kate Larsen

BookLeaf Publishing

Presentation by *BookLeaf Publishing*

Web: www.bookleafpub.com

E-mail: info@bookleafpub.com

ISBN: 9789357740630

First edition 2023

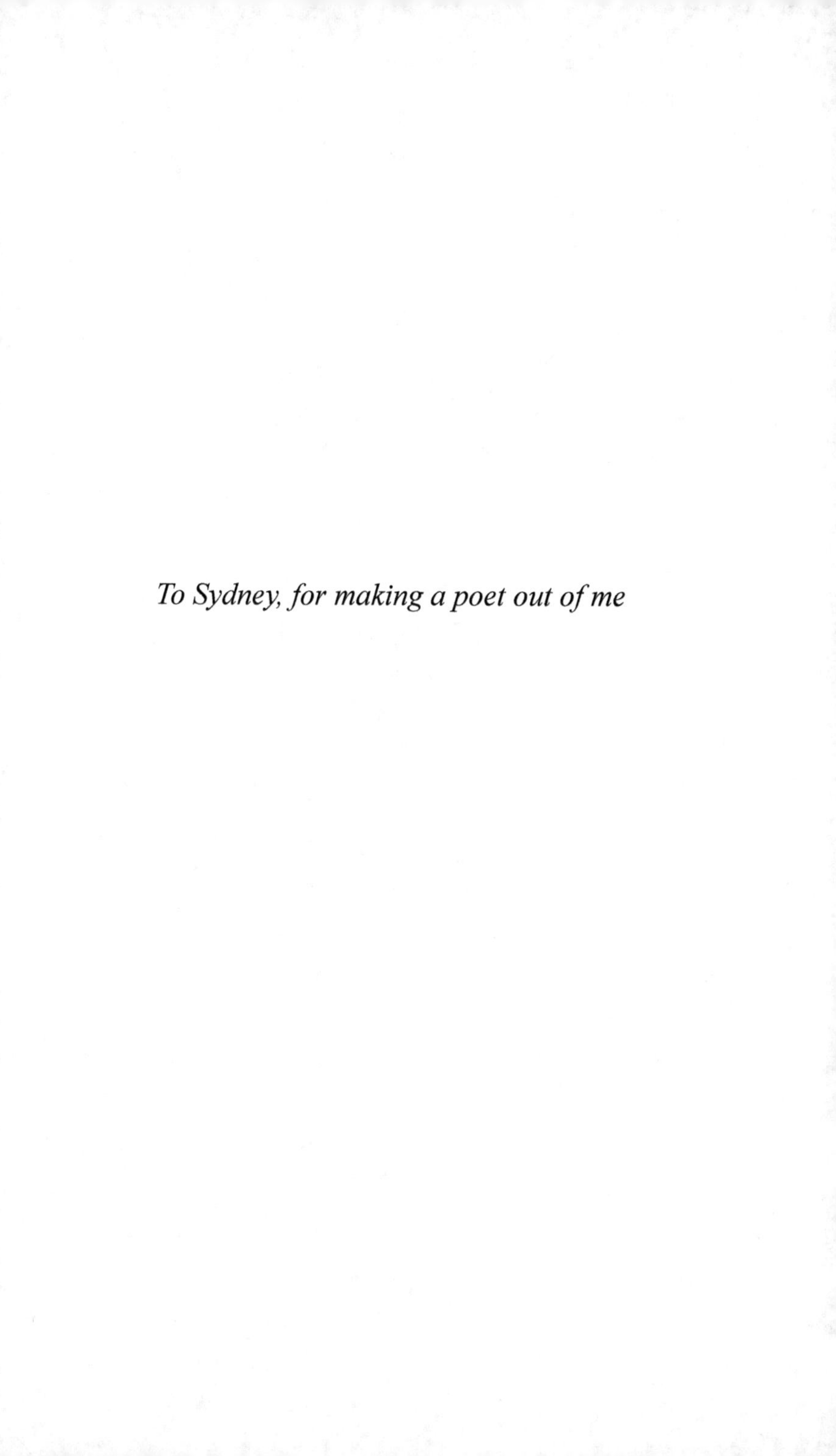

To Sydney, for making a poet out of me

ACKNOWLEDGEMENT

I'd like to thank my parents for encouraging me to write and my siblings for being so supportive. A huge thanks to Annie Hartman for helping with the cover design! You are seriously a life saver! Thank you to my beta reader Stephanie Gaudinier for helping me with the titles of my poems and getting me excited about this project again; your insight was invluable! And to everyone else who has supported me in my writing endeavors: with every ounce of my soul, thank you.

PREFACE

TW: blood, violent themes

a recomposition

It's your fault,
really—burying yourself beneath a paper
headstone.
Too easy for me to tear from the earth,
grin at its weeping streaks of ink
because you were foolish enough to forget the
rain
before you died.

I clawed the crumpled mass to tatters,
and blew the scraps into the wind like dandelion
seeds—
I wished to forget you
even as I dug up your carcass, sucking on worms
while I worked,
breaking my jaw
on soil-pebbles.

That's me, the grave robber.
Here to spread the dust of your bones
thin across my weary desk, spell metaphors with
the grains.
I'd have liked the look of you fresh (blood
makes for pretty stains),
but no matter—any stage of decomposed will
suffice:

Bone-dust, blood, bloated flesh, tender muscle—
fodder for my flame-songs, scent
to my putrid poetry.

silt

3

enough dust collects on the riverbed
for me to mold the shape of your mind.
i wish the pieces of you
wouldn't scatter themselves with the current—
      a trail of blood leads to emptiness
      far too often

ceramic

this that drips from my eyes
is not tears. *(honey-thick)*
(ocean brine)
tints my vision tangerine.

it sits at the back of my throat, sweet
with mellow regret,
yellow decay.

you've claimed lavender—
dying orchids, your tears.
could you prove we aren't both
an untethered chaos?

perhaps the gold will dry cracked against my
cheeks,
pressed in by gentle sun-fingers—
my skin is like ceramic too
stressed
to keep from falling to pieces.
if i'm lucky, my fractures will glow heaven-like.

or perhaps i will forever remain rotting,
the steady dripping of the sweet stuff a reminder
of the sick behind my eyes.

even then, i know you'd stay.
violet tears, violent
against your skin.
we are breaking together—
ceramic people not meant
for this firing.

silver thread

catching the light of a sun
on the horizon.

this is how i imagine love.

the fragility of it—

i am learning this

with time.

scream

i swallowed a map of glass;
it tore my throat on its way to my chest.
the blood churned like a tempest
and smelled like early-morning rain

my larynx pressed eroding keys,
played the high notes,
and they escaped down a written path
to where my tongue stained the soil at my feet

fingertips raked at the tunnel they dug,
their sound like drums in the back of my head—
a rhythm to keep time to
while lily petals wither
and graveyards grow

the anchor that drowns us

there is heaviness in change.
thrill, too.

most times, it is sudden,
subtle:
painted nails, trimmed
hair.

other times, it is
leaving an island behind.

there is mourning in it.
anticipation, too.

but for all the islands shrinking
in our pupils,
the heaviness stays
and we hold on tightly
because the grief gives us a shred
of hope

that ties our souls to the gate of yesterday
so change is barred
from tomorrow's door.

censor

a wine bottle shatters, blood-red spilling
across the cold tile floor.
everybody stares, everybody looks away
pretending a piece of the glass
has not embedded itself in their hearts.

we are a zoo of animals in rib cages,
covered in red linen
to keep visitors' eyes bright and empty,
their minds unaltered.
> sometimes, a hand
> reaches blindly through the bars—
> the fingers latching onto frigid air
> before pulling away.

> the ensuing silence is enough to know
> they've gleaned a part of us
> and wish they hadn't.

so they force their fingers to forget,
and sculpt us
structures of the mind.

nothing more.

time lapse

desert sunsets wilt,
lightning, veins across velvet—
lips part, then grow cold.

behind the eyes

there is simplicity
in the silver-framed glass that reflects a stranger
in my clothes—
ease in the way i furrow my brow, cock my
head,

turn

away.

i looked at my face today and saw a star
collapse.
i wanted constellations.

why do we craft ourselves a steel rod
to cling to every inch of the way
before the shriveling?
what if we stepped away,
into the darkness where there is no sure
handhold, no clear
understanding of our worth
in the gazes of the people around us?

we craft palaces to hold above our heads, only
for them to tumble toward our skulls, crush

us. but we brush
off the dust,
ignore our scattered limbs and the
bloody

                                              trails

between.

others dare to notice.
they click their tongues, say:
what a mess your viscera makes

why is there always a calculation behind the
eyes that puppet the mouth?
perhaps the glass has a hold on them, too—
found its way down their throat
and lodged there, forcing toxic air from their lips
for all of us to inhale,
flutter our eyelids,
forget what a galaxy is
so we can't expect it
the next time we look
into our own eyes.

a poet's process of decay

i died today.

nothing sad, i swear.
it was a peaceful passing. warm.
my heart constricted one last time,
my muscles tightened in resistance to the
coming rest.
i couldn't blame them—what is anything
without a purpose?

my eyes were relieved.
they gave me colors,
soft and pastel. *rest,* they said, *at last.*

my ears crept uncertainly
around the quiet. they still whisper to me,
sometimes:
words once lost to memory.

my hair drooped—thick and heavy with grease
and regret. It told me nothing.
perhaps it never will.

my fingers still hiss at me–
theirs is the only sadness i carry in death.

their joints strain, their muscles protest,
their bones yearn for wind to mimic movement
again.

but this is the torture i bear–
a musician, a typist, whose fingers played her
melodies
to coax comfort from.
no peace for them now—they are restless
without work.

    the earth is heavy, but it is soft,
    fine, a caress over my uneasy bones.
    perhaps i can endure this after all.

    i wonder if there will ever come a day
    i lose sense of myself
    completely.

interlude

15

here is light–
a flicker, true.
but enough.

a whispering promise moving
with the faint breeze–
it tickles your ears,
smooths the rough edges of your
soul
just slightly.

this has all been violent,
hasn't it? so
take this matchstick–
let it remind you
not all is blood and tears and
pain.

there is joy like this–
such that even a flicker
can penetrate
despair.

this must be how the ocean feels

you weren't there
when the lamplight dimmed behind my
curtained eyelids.
> but you were the reason.

you weren't there when my heart grew chains
and sank, swiftly,
to a jagged rocky floor.

does it take distance for you to forget your
compassion?
does it take miles between us
for you to become the tear-drop people
i used to hide from inside my skin?

this must be how the ocean feels
when a steam-powered ship cuts through its
current.
> powerless, fearful,
>> small.

i create oceans for you here—
it would hurt me more than anything to see you
drown in them.

i'd much prefer to teach you to float
if you'd cut the engine,
sit in the itchy silence,

listen.
please,
      listen.

the emptiness   is loud,

uncomfortable,

     and i'm   tired

of shielding   you

     from   it.

falter

i am stilettos
on wire, strung out over this
trembling aorta.

tasteless

hear the colors deep in my pupils
and say the sound is sadder than
sunlight.

wrap me in shadows, and tell me
they're stars. i'd believe you
even if your words were stalactites, pointed and
dripping
with spite. perhaps there is a desperation
beyond that of the starving one—
there is more that could be said
about the way we feel the salt
in our ears, but never reach to scoop it away.

yet
there are cavities i wouldn't enter—
footsteps i wouldn't follow, trees i wouldn't
want
to learn from. there are oceans
that would drown me, and i know them.

replace my heart with brick,
i'd taste the weight and sweeten it–
soften it to muscle–
ignoring the bitterness of your hovering tongue.

perhaps you've already sunk
beneath tasteless waters
and that is why you reach for me,
chains in hand.

centipede

i knew a girl
who peeled the memories from her head,
wound them around a cold, rusty wheel.
her eyes, like projector lights
shone on the crumbling plaster wall
and she'd watch Past
scuttle across her irises—
a centipede on the screen.

i knew a girl
whose legs grew stiff,
whose spine bent willow-like,
whose eyes became deserts,
whose palms bled
and kept bleeding.

who searched for joy
in the ghost of smiles,
wished for recycled time
on dying stars,

who slept counting
the legs of the centipede,
repeating its names,
its skeletons,

until her lips cracked.

i saw the deadness
in the creature's eyes,
the poison streaked
across its teeth, the smoke
curling around its body–
but seeing the tendrils around her wrists,
the resolve settling under her skin,
my lips never parted to warn her.
i turned away,
let her roots find soil in dusty reels of film,

and left the centipede to dance.

viridian

i guess
i'm the person
who keeps wilted roses
on the windowsill
because i see beauty
in their cold, crisp death.

everything around me fades
to green,
myself most of all.
so i fall to the ground
at some hollow well,
because there can't be such a thing
as emptiness:
if so with roses, it is so with me.

the color is too much,
too much green,
but it has seared itself
into the dark corners of my brain
and its hungry flame
triggers the rapid beating
of a pair of skin drums.

the lights are off, the color is not

and i wish for falling petals
to swallow the nothingness.

firefly

a firefly buzzes in my skull,
bouncing aimlessly against the silky bone,
soaking its light in the fleshy mass of my brain.

my neurons don't know what to do with it,
this insect trapped in a dark place with only the mind
to bring to light.
they fire away and i am twitching–
my skin throbs.
i adjust the collar of my shirt, but still it feels
like a shovel in my skin.

i don't like the burrowing.

the fear doesn't translate to my hands–
i'm not one for trembling.
i'm not one for panicking either
(sometimes i wonder if that makes me human at all).

there still remains the problem of my youth.
will my brain stifle the insect with its growth?
shed its immature cocoon and crush the thing?

if so, will its light burn out slowly
like a candle wick, or blink away
like an LED, submissive to the switch?

i am one for shuddering on occasion.
the buzzing itches my scalp,
tingles the follicles beneath my skin,
reminds me i need to wash my hair in the
morning.
reminds me why i won't be happy in the
morning.

i've created a prison,
walled in the thing that flies,
knowing its innocence but not knowing what
else to do with it.

there—
a flicker reflective of my uncertainty.
i've always been one to flicker.

i keep my skull a glass jar, for now
(this is how i pretend i have any choice in the
matter at all).

code

i have this book with gold-leaf pages.
it's supposed to be poetry—some sort of caboose
hauling verses toward Horizon(Mirage).

i don't know what to do with them—the pages.
i flip through them at random and the paper falls
to dust at my touch,
but sometimes i catch words, ink fluttering,
meaningless–
empty eyes in some crowded, smoky place.

they're supposed to form metaphors. the
blinking means something
but i haven't learned the code yet, my typewriter
fingers are cold
and instead i turn my head to the rattling
windows of this aimless train—
i sit in a boxcar littered with paper scraps and
fingernails.

tendrils of Mist(Nightmare) curl around
everything
and i think i see flecks of gold in there
somewhere—

the air sits patient beside me and sweat makes
camp above my lip.
the caboose is right there, behind me out the
window, empty and blinking.
it tells me to search the dust that settles itself
behind my eyes, stuffs itself into my cheeks—
but i haven't learned the code yet,
so i shake the grains from my head and pull my
gaze away.

voice

i am wading through glass,
shards up to my knees, and i still delve deeper
because there is nowhere else to go.

i am afraid to open my mouth for fear of
damaging my tongue—
i will let my shins be cut to ribbons before I lose
my
voice.

my lips are parched, split down the middle and
wishing
for a reason to part, impart a plea for pardon,
but there is no one to scream to, no one to take
my tongue for what it's worth.

something misfired in my nerves, i think.
the pain has silenced itself—lost its voice,
perhaps, from all the screaming.
still, enough lingers for me to remember the
ghost of it:

a hand with enough force to touch the skin and
break it,

spoon out the blood and let it run curiously
through its fingers while i stare
at the mouths of tapered skin, knowing their
screams had they any lungs.

i donated mine a while ago—lungs, i mean.
i still feel the print of them in my chest. another
trick of the mind:
pretending i could sigh, and someone

would
hear.

paper people

i am surrounded by
paper faces
penciled smiles, inky eyes
unblinking, unthinking

they stretch forth wrinkled hands,
      blue lines everywhere
      blanks space, emptiness,
      everywhere

i am glue or glitter or staple
to them—
symbol of a connection unreachable
with their organs fumbled, flattened, folded
away…

or maybe mirrors
show us the flesh, the filled-in places
to mask the thin emptiness that coats us like
paint.
maybe none of us are skin at all
and we are all just paper people—
      filling ourselves with fantasy
      instead of ink-thick blood

a moment

Here is calm—
a breath, steamy
in the knife-like air.

A moment.

All things
come to an end,
even the painful ones,
to make way
for peace–

Even
if it is but a suspense in time—
a cloud of breath
to dissipate in seconds against the cold—
it is still a sigh.

It is still relief.